To: CArty + the CArty
Children

GOD Bless you and
your family
keep up the great work
in the WRD

Love you

A God of
Second Chances

Revived by
God

Nieasia N. Wilkins

WESTBOW
PRESS®
A DIVISION OF THOMAS NELSON
& ZONDERVAN

This book is a work of non-fiction. Unless otherwise noted, the author and the publisher
make no explicit guarantees as to the accuracy of the information contained in this book
and in some cases, names of people and places have been altered to protect their privacy.

WestBow Press books may be ordered through booksellers or by contacting:

WestBow Press
A Division of Thomas Nelson & Zondervan
1663 Liberty Drive
Bloomington, IN 47403
www.westbowpress.com
844-714-3454

Because of the dynamic nature of the Internet, any web addresses or links contained in
this book may have changed since publication and may no longer be valid. The views
expressed in this work are solely those of the author and do not necessarily reflect the
views of the publisher, and the publisher hereby disclaims any responsibility for them.

Any people depicted in stock imagery provided by Getty Images are
models, and such images are being used for illustrative purposes only.
Certain stock imagery © Getty Images.

Scripture quotations marked KJV are taken from the King James Version.

Scripture quotations marked NIV are taken from The Holy Bible, New
International Version®, NIV® Copyright © 1973, 1978, 1984, 2011 by
Biblica, Inc.® Used by permission. All rights reserved worldwide.

ISBN: 978-1-6642-6755-8 (sc)
ISBN: 978-1-6642-6756-5 (hc)
ISBN: 978-1-6642-6754-1 (e)

Library of Congress Control Number: 2022909530

Print information available on the last page.

WestBow Press rev. date: 6/21/2022

CONTENTS

Acknowledgments ix

Introduction xiii

Chapter 1   Teenage Years 1

Chapter 2   Love Doesn't Hurt 13

Chapter 3   Jesus Heals! 31

Chapter 4   Words to the Wise 53

Chapter 5   Salvation 83

Love Letter

To Jesus Christ, Father God, and the Holy Ghost. Thank you for your existence. Lord, If it wasn't for you saving me, I wouldn't have a story to tell. You made it possible for me to be here. Jesus Christ, you have taken me from the pit in one of the darkest hours of my life and touch me with your love. I thank you, my Lord, for not allowing me to die in my sin. You coming into my life changed my life forever for eternity. I acknowledge you, my Lord, for all you have done for my daughters and me. I am so grateful to have you as my Lord of Lords and King of Kings forever. Thank you, and I love you, my Lord, forever and ever. Amen.

Love,

Nieasia

ACKNOWLEDGMENTS

To my Lord and Savior Jesus Christ, my Father God, and the Holy Ghost, without your existence I would not exist. I thank you for being the love, light, and joy of my life. Thank you for making our book come forth to the light. I am grateful to you for being my healer, Dr. Jesus Christ, and for showing me your unconditional love. Your compassion and love are what drew me into you. Thank you. I love you, my Lord.

To my two beautiful daughters, thank you for being a help to me even when you didn't know you were doing so.

Thank you for putting a smile on my face even through the tough times and tears. You were my smile that kept me pushing forward to fight to want to live. I love you.

To my mom, thank you for being a blessing to me during one of the darkest hours of my life and letting me know to give everything to God. Thank you for being a light and sharing the most important love of my life to me—Jesus Christ and Father God—even when I didn't understand. Thank you for being understanding. I love you, Mom.

To Late Bishop Foy and Mother Foy, who went on to be with the Lord: you were truly a blessing from the Lord. I thank God for you sharing the truth and the living by the Word of God. Bishop Foy and Mother Foy, thank you for praying for me and letting me know to put Father God first and obey him in all that I do. I love you.

To the Emmanuel Church of Christ Disciple of Christ family prayer warriors—Sister Glover, Mother Holly, Deacon Regan, Brother Taylor, Pastor Sutton, Late Brother George and—thank you for showing your support and love. Thank you for welcoming my daughters and me into your family and showing love.

To my sister in Christ Jesus Evangelist Wilson, thank you for being there for me even through the painful times. Thank you for praying for me and lifting me up daily to the Lord. Thank you for showing love and compassion to me even when I was down. I love you.

To Minister Williams, I thank you for being my book & life coach and your Late husband for being a blessing to me and praying for me in a tough season in my life. Thank for inviting me to your second home the bible store Crossroads of Life in Hillside, NJ. Thank you for your words of wisdom and the coaching experience.

Thank you for allowing God to pour into you so you could pour into me to help me see the heart of God come to pass. God bless you

To Prophetess Joy, thank you for being my mentor and believing in me and encouraging me to go high in the Lord. I thank you for allowing God to use you to speak into my life. God bless you

To Abundant Life Worship Church, where the late Pastor Joe was and which now is led by Pastor Donnie, Pastor Bruno, and Sis Debbie: thank you for your teachings on how to live in a holy way for the Lord, and thank you for all your prayers.

INTRODUCTION

The spirit of the Lord used a friend of mine, Reverend Vivian, to let me know I was to write this book. The first thing I thought was "Who, me?" Before the spirit of the Lord shared this, I could not even get a complete sentence down or get into a good class. I looked at my situation in a natural way because of what I was going through, even though I was told of the book. The Lord allowed me to know it was him blessing me to tell my story of Jesus Christ's testimony for his glory.

This is a book about a young teenager that makes bad choices at an early age. She has to grow up very early in life because of the decisions she makes. As she goes on in life, she witnesses some things that she doesn't like. In her home, she deals with a lot of stress, feeling unliked, misunderstood, mistreated, and hurt. She thinks anywhere else she goes will better than where she is. So she looks for love on the outside and she meets up with some people she thinks care for her. Those people then begin to use her for what they can get. She really doesn't know what she is getting herself into. She gets hurt and abused. Then she tries to get herself back on track. She happens to be at the wrong place at the wrong time and meets someone she thinks she can trust and falls into a trap. She goes back to the place where she knows it's hard for her to go. At that time, her mother tells her some valuable key information that will help her in her life.

CHAPTER 1
Teenage Years

The reason I am sharing these things with you is because I am a firm believer that we all can learn from other people's mistakes. We can take the things that the Lord brings us through and help someone else by the grace of God. I was not just healed and saved just for myself. My life was spared that I might help others who are hurting and want to be loved. I was called to be a blessing to share Jesus Christ, and I believe that this will help you too.

Here is my story.

I grew up in a single-parent home, and my mom had to work all the time. She was constantly out providing and working hard for her family. So we didn't get to talk much about life, and we didn't get a chance to have the mom-and-daughter talk that is common in so many families. When my mom wasn't around, I found myself getting into a lot of trouble and getting into things that only married couples are normally involved in. I met a individual and knew very little about him. Not too long after that, I found out I was pregnant. I was a young teenager at the time and was too nervous to let anyone know, so I hid my pregnancy for six months. This wasn't the smartest thing on my part. When it came to me letting my mom know, I was afraid of what my mom might think or say, as any teenager would be if he or she were to do something wrong or fall short. I was like this because I valued her opinion.

On the other hand, you can imagine what my mom thought. I was one of her young teenagers and was having a baby. She didn't expect me to be having a baby at this age, and I wasn't finished with high school yet. I was in my sophomore year of high school and was in the beginning stages of my courses. Also, I wasn't someone she would expect to give her any problems or issues. My mom didn't want me to follow in her footsteps.

She was a single parent of nine kids and doing it all by herself, trying to do the best she could for everyone. She wouldn't think for even a moment that I would be having a baby. Also, I had seen how hard she had to work to put food on the table and take care of kids. I hadn't thought about what might happen to me if I had a baby at this age. It looked from my view as though I was in my own little world, as to some degree I thought it was all right in my eyes because I was with this guy.

Soon reality set in. I had a lot of things running through my mind. How was I going to let my mom know? How was I going to provide for and protect my baby? I was a teenager having my first baby, and I didn't know the first thing about raising a child. I didn't have a job, so I could not afford to take care of a baby. I went from having no responsibilities to having a lot of responsibilities as a teenager. I went from having no accountability to having accountability. I could not think about myself first anymore; I had to think about having my baby first.

During this time in my life, I had to grow up really fast, and I wasn't prepared for what I had to deal with in life (adult issues). I had to deal with a lot of physical and emotional issues and problems (grown-up issues) that I caused for myself. I was clueless regarding some of the things that were happening to my body, but this was life for me. It seemed to be too much for me to handle at one time, and I couldn't talk to anybody about it. It was physically and emotionally draining for me at the time. Even though I didn't understand a lot of things, it seemed as if God were showing me something and covering me at the same time. What I learned was that God will reveal to us what's going on in a particular situation. Also, he will show us what's to come if we continue to go in that path. "He will do this to get our attention an to protect us."

After going through these things, I didn't think there was any hope for me because of what I was seeing and hearing and what I had gotten myself into. I felt as though my life were over. I felt as if I had failed and was an odd teenager in life because of the poor choices I had made. Also, at this time in my life, the individual that I was with and I hadn't been around each other for very long. I believe that security and trust are very important to have in any type of relationship. If I felt as if that security and trust were broken, it wasn't good, and I didn't have a sense of protection. If I didn't have that protection and trust, it was over with, one way or another. Around this time, it seemed as though everything was coming at me all at once, which felt overwhelming. All I knew was that I needed some help.

During my teenage years, it seemed as if everything I did was wrong where I lived. It didn't matter how well I tried to do things; I was always in the wrong. I didn't hear anything good spoken about me. I felt as if I was misunderstood a lot and as if I were an odd person. A lot of times I didn't get asked to do things but would be put in a situation where I had to do them no matter whether they felt overwhelming or not. Instead of people asking me how I felt or what I thought, they wanted to tell me what I was thinking. I surely didn't have a voice, and when I did speak, I was in the wrong. By this time I needed life speaking over me and not death, no matter how much of a mess I was in, no matter how bad I was, and no matter how bad my situation looked. Proverbs 18:21 (KJV) says, "Death and life are in the power of the tongue: they that love it shall eat the fruit thereof." I needed positive and not negative words spoken over me. I needed encouragement and not discouragement. I constantly found myself getting into arguments, so when it came time for someone to have a serious talk with me, I didn't want to hear it; I was rebellious and didn't want to listen. "It seemed as if I was given up on and without hope, even though people had probably meant well, but God." I was hurting at the time but didn't know how to talk about it.

One way I did to show that I was hurting was change my actions. Around that time, I didn't feel as though I was getting shown love from anywhere. So I went out and stayed out, and I started hanging around people who accepted me for who I was. I didn't care who I was with or where I was; I just wanted love and peace of mind. I hung out on the streets and at friends' places because I didn't want to be in a place of getting torn and overwhelmed. While I was out on streets, I was also at other friends' places and didn't see other strangers coming into their homes and interrupting their households. In these places, I saw that things were a little different from where I was living, and I was okay with that. It wasn't perfect but it wasn't chaotic. While I was out on the streets, the friends who accepted me were the ones who I thought cared for me. The friends who I thought cared for me are the ones that used me for what they could get out of me sexually. All they wanted was to keep me by their side for pleasure and for me to be their sidepiece. The love that I thought I was getting ended up being lust. I learned that the hard way.

As a teenager, I made some unwise decisions, but I'm here to let you know to be careful not to move so quickly. The grass is not greener on the other side. Everything is not what it always seems to be. You might be going through some similar things in your home, and you might feel as if you need to look for love on the outside or look for love in other places. Don't be so quick as to leave before your time. No one place is perfect or without any issues or problems. Pray about it and give it to the Lord Jesus Christ. If you are hurting and don't know what to say to the Lord, look at Matthew 6:9–13 (KJV). The Word says, "After this manner therefore pray ye: Our Father which art in heaven, Hallowed be thy name. Thy kingdom come, Thy will be done in earth, as it is in heaven. Give us this day our daily bread. And forgive us our debts, as we forgive our debtors. And lead us not unto temptation, but deliver us from evil: For thine is the kingdom, and the power, and the glory, forever. Amen." Jesus will hear you. Let him help you and guide you; you're not too young or too old for God to talk to you or help you. The mistake I made was seeking love on the outside, and it didn't work; it was only temporary lust.

CHAPTER 2
Love Doesn't Hurt

I often found myself in unhealthy relationships. Instead of giving myself time to breathe or think about what kind of relationship I was in, I got into another one, thinking, *This one is okay.* I didn't think too much about it. I learned some things over time; one of them is that we really need to get to know an individual before dealing with him or her. As ladies and gentleman, we can't continue to rush things that are a process. Even when a person does a lot of sweet-talking, charming, and being very nice, it's always best to get to know an individual. Moving too quickly can end up in a baby coming into the picture, or some type of bonding. I know because it happened to me.

These are signs you can look for in unhealthy relationships with an individual:

- The person is always unstable.

- The person is verbally or physically abusive.
- The person apologizes over and over but you don't see a change in his or her behavior.

I decided I didn't want to live in an unhealthy relationship any longer. I'd had an enough of everything, and I was tired. This was the lifestyle that I lived; this was what I knew. I didn't know any other way, but I knew something was wrong when it kept on happening to me over and over. At that point, I knew love shouldn't hurt; that was my last straw. I didn't want to be in an unhealthy relationship any longer.

During this time, I was mostly out with friends, but I would always attract the wrong crowd of people to me. These were the ones that would say they wanted to be with me but had hidden motives. I didn't like being cheated on, I didn't like sharing a boyfriend, and I didn't like being misused. Yes, I was unwise and gullible at the time, but I thought the people I was around had my best interest in mind.

In these situations, I was always told "I love you" by someone, but I was told that to get one thing—sex. Because I thought that I was cared about and loved, I allowed myself to be used and abused. At first this was not what I was seeing out in the world, but it started happening to me over and over. I was blind to what I was allowing to happen to me. I would put myself in these situations, and I would always get hurt emotionally and physically. I am reminded that 1 Corinthians 13:4–7 (NIV) says, "Love is patient, love is kind. It does not envy, it does not boast, it is not proud. It does not dishonor others, it is not self-seeking, it is not easily angered, it keeps no record of wrongs. Love does not delight in evil but rejoices with the truth. It always protects, always trust, always hopes, always perseveres."

One of the things God will show us if we are paying close attention to him is the truth about an individual if we really want to know. Sometimes we may say, "But God, he is so nice; but God, he bought me these name-brand clothes; but God, he has all this money; but God, we are a match made in heaven." Sometimes we tell God these things as though he doesn't know about the individual in question. But God already knows everything about the individual, even the deeper things about him or her. Are we really ready for the truth that God wants to

show us? That is the question! John 8:32 (KJV) Jesus said, "ye shall know the truth and the truth shall make you free." When you know the truth it's going to save your life. When you walk in truth it's going to save you some heartache. "When you obey the truth it's going to set you free." Not that any person is perfect; there is none perfect except Jesus and God. God will give us signs and warnings to protect us and let us know we don't have to go that route. We don't have to go that way, and we don't have to go into that lane. He will give us a spiritual GPS that will never die out, and it will never take us over a cliff. That spiritual GPS is the Holy Spirit, which will guide us into all truth. What the Lord says to us will save us a lot of trouble if we are obedient to him and follow his directions.

Teenager Spiritual Alert 1

Young women, if you are in a relationship and you being physically abused, the best thing to do is leave. A real man will not beat on you. A real man will not cheat on you. Some guys will tell you, "You ain't worth it," and they may say you can't leave them because you have no place to go, you need them, you can't make it on your own, or no one else will find you attractive. I am here to tell you such words come from a lying spirit from the pit of hell. It is trying to get you to stay in that place and trying to keep you in bondage. That spirit is trying to bring you down so you will feel bad, hopeless, worthless, and depressed. Don't sit there and keep on allowing that person to keep verbally and physically abusing you. It's not worth it! There are leaders in the churches today that can pray with you and help you. You don't have to stay in the midst of that mess. You deserve better; don't allow yourself to get beaten up anymore. One of the best things you can do for yourself and the other person is to help yourself to get out of that situation. After the first time he puts his hands on you and keep on doing it and then tells you he is sorry, it's not worth staying with that person. It's not even worth arguing with the person. The person is not being remorseful. No one should take abuse from anyone. If a person says he or she loves you, that person should do his or her best to make sure that you are safe and should not harm you. God didn't put us here to be anybody's punching bag. Getting punched by someone is not right, and it's not okay.

This is summed up in the following poem I wrote:

Teenagers and young women,

Why put yourself in that predicament?

You don't have to go through that unnecessary drama.

Separate yourself from that trouble.

Why be in the midst of the name-calling?

Why take the abuse?

Why be in a place where you are not wanted?

Why trouble yourself an get stressed out?

Come out from among that stuff.

Come out from the midst of that place.

You don't have to stay in the midst of that mess.

You can do better by the grace of God,

By prayer, and by moving when God says, "Move."

Continue to put your trust in him,

and let the Holy Spirit lead you.

"The Lord will never leave you nor forsake you."

After going through these situations, I began to wonder, "Why am I here? Is there any hope for me? Why am I getting into the same situation over and over?" I didn't like feeling this way. Sometimes I felt worthless, and I was tired. I just wanted to do better for my daughters, but I didn't know how. I still had the same issues and the same problems. I didn't like it. So again I constantly ran the streets, which was not good on my part, because I just created more problems for myself. I had serious problems, because I was ending up in the same predicament.

I went on to continue with the same type of lifestyle that I had been living. I had the same old habits. I did want better, but it looked as if doing better was hard. I had issues but didn't know how to resolve them. I did what I knew how to do—running the streets as though there was no tomorrow. At the time, I just wanted to go out, and that's what I did. While I was out there again, the wrong people would try to gravitate toward me.

One of those nights, I was out with friends in the wrong place at the wrong time with a person, and I was misled and deceived. After some time passed, I began to get sick; I was stressed and worried. It took a toll on my body. I went back and forth to various doctors, and they weren't sure what was going on. I was scared and anxious about everything. I knew I was dealing with a lot of things physically and emotionally. It was too much for me to handle. I was tired and exhausted. I felt as if I were going to leave this earth!

Turning Point

During that time, I was given a book of scriptures—the Word of God. I kept reading the Word of God. The Word of God helped me to stay calm. It gave me a peace that I could not explain at the time. Not that I wasn't going through anything; I had issues and problems, but only by God's grace did I feel his peace. Philippians 4:7 (KJV) says, "And the peace of God, which passeth all understanding, shall keep your hearts and minds through Jesus Christ." And that's what the Word of God did for me. God was with me even during this time, and I didn't know it. As time went on, the Lord used someone to let me to know that. John 1:4 (KJV) says, "This sickness is not unto death, but for the glory of God, that the son of God might be glorified thereby."

Teenage Spiritual Alert 2

Teenagers and young women, listen to the warnings that the Lord gives you. I don't care if you don't have a relationship with the Lord yet. The Lord still will give you warnings, because he cares for you, even if you are out in the world. He knows his children, and he wants the best for them. Even when a person is still out in the world doing whatever he or she wants, God will still try to get that person's attention. We may say to God, "Oh God, he cares for me. Oh God, he takes me out. Oh God, he shows me affection."

Father God shows us things because he sees everything we don't see. He sees in the spiritual realm. God will see the evil spirit that a person is carrying, and he will give us a warning so we won't go with the individual. God sees everything, but we may not receive his warning and may go with the individual he is trying to warn us about. God allows this to happen because we have free will. He does not intend to harm us; he simply wants to show us when a choice isn't good for us. With all that having been said, God is a just God. God bestows grace and mercy on us in the midst of our messes even when we are near to destroying ourselves. God shows us that he was keeping us and protecting us because He loves and cares for us. The Lord protects his people even in the mist of their messes, and he does so because he loves us. It doesn't matter how many times the devil tries to set us up or how many mistakes we make; the Lord will still give us warnings. Romans 5:8 (KJV) says, "But God commendeth his love toward us, in that, while we were yet sinners, Christ died for us." That is how much the Lord loves us.

Reflections

What have you learned from reading these chapters so far?

_____

_____

_____

_____

What are some of the warnings that God gives to us?

_____

_____

_____

_____

I Needed Help

I needed help, and it was not the sort of help anyone could give me; only Jesus could help me. One day I was sitting next to my mom, and she said, "Give it all to God." She meant well, but at the time I didn't understand what she meant. She said, "God can help you," and I waved and walked away because I really didn't understand. Even though I grew up going to church every Sunday, I was baptized when I was a kid, and I was taught and read about the love stories of Jesus and Father God, I just didn't have a personal relationship with him at the time; I did not know much about him. It was not that I didn't love Jesus and God; I just didn't have that intimate relationship with him at the time. It was religion, and I didn't know much about relationships. As time went on, I got increasingly tired until I felt I could not go on. I was just tired of life—too tired to live.

My mom invited me to come out with her to a prayer meeting service. Weeks later, I took the step and went with her. At this time in my life, I was in a very dark place. Yes, the lights were on in the church, but I was in a very dark place in my life. It was dark around me. I just sat in back, listening to the Word that was being spoken. No one bothered me. The deacons prayed for a while. Then I saw people testifying to the glory of God. I remember hearing the men and women of God giving their testimony about a man named Jesus and how he saved, healed, delivered, and provided, as well as how the Lord blessed them over and over. Several weeks went by, and I kept hearing these great testimonies. Every time I came out to church, I heard about this man named Jesus Christ. He was well known there among the saints, and they were smiling while testifying about him. I was sitting there thinking that I wanted to know more about this man named Jesus Christ. I heard of awesome healings and deliverances that he did. I was interested in Jesus Christ, and from right there Jesus drew me into his love.

CHAPTER 3
Jesus Heals!

Every week I went to prayer meeting service, someone was given a testimony of how the Lord gave him or her strength, healed him or her, and blessed him or her. I began to pray and repent, and I asked God to help me. I wanted this pain to go away. I cried out to the Lord. I continued to pray and asked God to save me. And the Lord did. Psalm 34:6 (KJV) says, "This poor man cried, and the Lord heard him, and saved him out of all his troubles." And that's what the Lord did for me, too. One night at prayer service, God sent his servant to me. He said, the Lord said he is going to heal you. I looked at him. The man didn't know me, but God did. I was grateful to the Lord because he had spoken life into me even though I didn't have a relationship with the Lord yet and hadn't given my life over to him. It was the Lord God of Israel that loved me so much to speak life unto me. For Jesus to tell me that I would live and not die that was enough for me to believe in him. So I kept on praying and going to prayer service. Isaiah 55:11 (KJV) says, "So shall God word be that goeth forth out of his mouth: it shall not return unto him void, but it shall accomplish that which God please, and it shall proper in the thing where to he send it."

I remember the day the Lord blew his breath into me like it was yesterday. I was lying down when I felt life enter me. His spirit had entered me, and he blew his breath on me. Jesus Christ touched me and healed my body with his blood, and no one else was around me but the Lord Jesus Christ. He touched me with his healing power, and from that point it got better and better for me every day. I began to receive my strength back and to feel better and relieved, and I had a peace over me. The sickness, stress, hurt, and anxiety left my body. The Lord healed and restored me. I felt as if I could live again, I felt like a brand new person. I also remember having a dream where God showed me that I could have died. If I had not repented and turned from my ways, I would not be here today. All along, God was protecting and watching over me.

Jesus Can Do the Same for You Too

God had grace and mercy on me. He gave me a second chance to get it right with him. If it wasn't for the Lord, I wouldn't be here today. I didn't do anything good in life to deserve God's healing. He is the faithful and merciful one. He could have let me go, but this was not his will. It is just as is said in Romans 9:15–16 (KJV): "For he saith to Moses, I will have mercy on whom I will have mercy, and I will have compassion on whom I will have compassion. So then it is not of him that willeth, nor of him that runneth, but of God that sheweth mercy." This is because God is God all by himself. Jesus Christ saved and healed me. I thank the Lord for not letting me die in my sin. I experience Jesus Christ for myself as Jehovah Rophe, the Lord my healer, my Savior, my keeper and more. Jesus Christ healed me, and I know that he can do the same for you. Isaiah 52:5 (KJV) says, "But he was wounded for our transgressions, he was bruised for our iniquities: the chastisement of our peace was upon him; and with his stripes we are healed." The Lord is the one who gave me life and the strength to go on. I repented, prayed, and continued to pray, and I believed what God had spoken into my life. I thank God for forgiveness too, if it wasn't for his forgiveness, I would not be here today. Ephesians 1:7 (KJV) says, "In whom we have redemption through his blood, the forgiveness of sins, according to the riches of his grace."

A little while after that, I accepted Jesus Christ as my Savior, and it was the best thing I ever did in my life. Jesus Christ changed my life for the better.

The Healing Power of God

The healing power that Jesus Christ healed me with is the same healing power that he used to heal the woman with the issue of blood. I am going to give you a little history about the woman with the issue of blood. According to Mark 5:25–29 (KJV), the woman with the issue of blood had been with a blood-related issue for twelve long years. This is a long time to be with an issue. This is a long time to be in pain and to be bleeding. I can tell you that when a person loses that much blood, it may result in having to have a blood transfusion, or death. So I understand why this woman got so desperate when she heard of Jesus Christ. I understand why this woman pressed on to get to Jesus. Besides, she had to have heard about the miracles that Jesus had done in Gilead, such as his having turned water into wine. She had to have heard about when Jesus healed two men possessed with devils. She had to have heard about

Jesus healing a man with palsy and forgiving him. Mark 5:27 (KJV) says, "The women with the issue of blood had heard of Jesus, and came in and press behind, and touched his garment." This woman was determined to see Jesus, for she said, "If I may touch but his clothes, I shall be whole." An after touching Jesus's garments, the woman's blood dried up in that same hour. The women with the issue of blood was healed with the healing power of Jesus Christ from that day forth. This is the same healing power that Jesus Christ can heal you with today. This is the same healing power that is available to each and every person out here if he or she would only believe and receive. Sometimes we have to press through to let Jesus know we want to be healed and want to be delivered and set free. Can we start believing in and receiving in the name of Jesus Christ today?

It was Jesus Christ's blood that saved me. As the song "I Know It Was the Blood" says,

I know it was the blood that saved me

one day that I was lost

Jesus died on the cross

I know it was the blood that saved me.

Jesus shed his blood for me and you, so we can live unto him. Romans 5:8–10 (KJV) says, "But God commendeth his love toward us, in that, while we were yet sinners, Christ died for us, Much more then, being now justified by his blood, we shall be saved from wrath through him. For if, when we were enemies, we were reconciled to God by the death of his Son, much more, being reconciled, we shall be saved by his life." I thank God for the life of his Son, Jesus Christ, and his precious blood, for without Jesus's blood we are nothing. Without his blood, we have no healing. Without his blood, how do we expect to forgive? He paid the ultimate a price for our sins. Jesus was obedient to his Father. Now when Father God sees us, he sees us through the blood of

Jesus Christ. "An this is because we were brought with an high, high and high price by Jesus Christ."

Life Lessons I Have Learned

1. God let me know that there is a better way to live. He let me know I didn't have to go seeking love from anywhere else because he is love and he loves me. John 3:1 (KJV) says, "Behold, what manner of love the Father hath bestowed upon us, that we should be called the sons and daughter of God." He loves us. Also, I don't have to allow my body to be used or taken advantage of, and I don't have to take verbal and physical abuse from anybody.

2. God let me know that, according to 2 Corinthians 5:17 (KJV), "I am a new creature in Christ Jesus old things are passed away; behold, all things are become new." I am going to give you an example of what this mean. Way before I gave my life to

Jesus Christ I used to be a depressed person who wore black on top of black clothes. I had worn the long black fingernails and listened to hardcore rock all the time. This is the phase that I went through in life. But when I accepted Jesus into my life and I got baptized, I came up as a new person. As time went on I noticed something different; I no longer wanted to do the same things I used to do. Now I felt joy within me, and not depression. I felt lighter and not heavy. I went from listening to hardcore music to music that encourages and uplifts me. Also, I saw the clouds and sky as though they were brand-new to me. It was as if I had been blind, but now I could see. Jesus had given me a different walk, talk, sight, and tune.

God wanted my heart then Holy Ghost begin to dress me. God showed me his love every day by teaching me his Word and his ways. He allowed me to know that I am his child and he loves me in spite of. Through this he let me know that I am someone valuable to him.

3. When God saved me, things got better for me. I looked at things from a different view. I saw things from a different perspective. He let me know that this life is not about me but rather is about the Lord. I learned that it's not the bad things a person says about me that count; it's how I respond and how I handle a situation. Also, the Lord taught me how to pray for people regardless of how I am treated. In the Matthew 5:44 (KJV), Jesus says, "Love your enemies, bless them that curse you, do good to them that hate you, and pray for them which despitefully use you, and persecute you."

God did it for me, and I know he can do the same for you without a shadow of doubt. "GOD is no respecter of persons." I learned it doesn't matter who you are or where you have been. God can take a nobody—a messed-up, sick person in any situation—and turn that person around to be used for his glory and story. It doesn't matter how bad it is or how it feels or what it looks like. God can save, deliver, and heal you. He is a loving, gracious God. "He doesn't wish that any shall perish." Jesus can save to the utmost.

Let's Change How We View Things

In order for us to see different results, we must do something different. In order for us to see a change, we must make a shift. We can do that by renewing our minds with the Word of God and acting on truth. Romans 12:2 (KJV) says, "And be not conformed to this world: but be ye transformed by the renewing of your mind, that ye may prove what is that good, and acceptable, and perfect, will of God." We really can't live as the world live their life. Our mindset has to change, and our view needs to be different. Can we see through the eyes of God? Can we see through the lenses of God? Philippians 2:5 (KJV) says, "Let this mind be in you that's in Christ Jesus." We need the mind of Christ. Can we ask God what it is to live by his Word? Then we need to obey him. Learn the Word of God and ask the Lord to help you to act upon it. We can't continue to live the same old lifestyle and expect the Lord's blessings to be upon us. When we hear and act upon his Word, we are walking in truth. But a person has to want to walk in truth. He will not force his ways on you. He is not that kind of God; Jesus is a gentleman. The decision is up to you.

Don't Give Up

Teenagers, there will probably be times in your life when you can talk to someone, and there will be times when you probably feel as if you are alone. But I am here to let you know your life is not over because you fell short of God. Romans 3:23 (KJV) says, "For all have sinned, and come short of the glory of God." And that's the Word. There is not one perfect person on this earth other than Jesus Christ. There are some things you may have control over and some things you may not have control over. There are things that happen in life when we make unwise choices and the unwise choices we make result in us dealing with the consequences of our actions. You may have made a couple of mistakes and poor choices. But I am here to let you know that you don't need to give up on life because you have a lot of things going on. Your life can change for the better, and you can start that process by choosing to make wise choices and godly decisions.

We Can All Learn from Our Mistakes

Your life is not over because you fell short of God's Word. Get back up and repent to the Lord and give everything over to him. Learn from your mistakes. I will say this again: learn from your mistakes. Don't keep on going around beating yourself up, thinking you have to keep living in the past and living that same old lifestyle. Get back up again! You can get through this with the help of the power of the Holy Ghost. I know that everything doesn't happen overnight, but it's a process, just as you didn't get into your previous situation overnight. There is nothing wrong with asking the Lord for help and repenting before him, but we can ask the Lord to help us through any situation; he is just waiting for us. Remember: he is a God of second chances.

Don't Listen

Don't listen to that lying voice that tells you that you can't come to the Lord because you fell short or committed a sin. You're not a failure; you're not a loser because you made mistakes and fell short in life. Don't listen to that defeated voice that tells you, you won't make it in life because you did something wrong. Jesus is not concerned about how many mistakes you made in your life or how many kids you had. He still loves you anyhow. Jesus is not counting how many bad things you did in your life. He still will accept you anyhow. You might think you are the worst person ever in the world, and guess what? The Lord still cares for you and loves you anyhow. For example, there are people out there that think that because they made mistakes they can't come to the Lord or attend church. Some people even think that they have to be cleansed or have it all together to come to the Lord. Proverbs 20:9 (KJV) says,

"Who can say, I have made my heart clean, I am pure from my sins." I am here to let you know Jesus Christ is the only one that can make you clean. Jesus is the only one that can make you pure. In the book of John 15:3 (KJV), Jesus said, "Now ye are clean through the word which he have spoken unto you." The Lord wants you the way you are. Jesus will meet you where you are. I don't care how much of a mess you are or where you have been; Jesus is still waiting for you to take that first step.

Next Step

Once you have accepted Jesus Christ as your Savior, you will need the power of the Holy Spirit to live a saved life. Ask God in Jesus's name for the Holy Spirit. One of the reasons Jesus came is because he knew that it was impossible for us to live right without having his Holy Spirit. Jesus says in John 14:26 (KJV), "But the

Comforter, which is the Holy Ghost, whom the Father will send in his name, he shall teach you all things, and bring all things to your remembrance, whatsoever he have said unto you." That's his Word. We need him for everything; we can't do it without Jesus Christ, Father God, and the Holy Ghost. God knew that we needed him; God knew we couldn't live without him, and God knew that we couldn't breathe without him. We can't build without him, we can't walk without him, and we can't even think without him. How do we expect to live on Earth without him? We can't. I know I can't. Thank you, Father God, Jesus Christ, and the Holy Ghost, for your directions.

Reflections

Do you believe Jesus can heal you?

_____

_____

_____

_____

How can we change a worldly mindset to an spiritual mindset? And what scripture we can meditate on to help us?

_____

_____

_____

_____

What life lessons have you learned from reading chapter 3?

_____

_____

_____

_____

CHAPTER 4
Words to the Wise

Teenagers, live your lives, enjoy your teenage years, and focus on doing well in school. Be careful not to jump into unhealthy relationships. Also be careful of jumping into relationships too quickly with people, because there will be plenty of opportunity as you get older. Before you know it, you will be an adult wishing you were younger and without issues, problems, or responsibility. Enjoy your teenage years and wait on the Lord, for he knows who and what are best for you.

Think before You Act

Teenagers, think about things before you do them. If a person is with someone sexually outside of marriage, there are consequences. There are consequences in our lives for our actions, whether good or bad. Having sex outside marriage is not healthy for the body at all, and a lot of things can happen to the body; there are risks. The world might tell you sex outside marriage is good and right. I am here to let you know that sex outside of marriage is not blessed. God designed sex for married couples. In 1 Corinthians 7:1–2 (KJV), the Lord uses the apostle Paul to say, " It is good for a man not to touch a woman. Nevertheless, to avoid fornication, let every man have his own wife, and let every woman have her own husband." And that's the Word.

You Are So Special

You might not know this, but you are someone special to the Lord, and he loves you with an everlasting love. One of the things he doesn't like is when we go against his Word, because when that happens, we separate ourselves from our Lord Jesus Christ and Father God. Can you understand why our Father God doesn't like it when we go against his Word? He doesn't want to be separated from his children; he wants to be close to us and have an intimate relationship with us, For he is a holy God. In 1 Peter 1:15–16 (KJV) we read, "But as he which hath called you is holy, so be ye holy in all manner of conversation; Because it is written, Be ye holy; for I am holy." Our Father God wants us to dwell with him because he loves us.

We are a special people that have a greater purpose in God.

Let me share with you how special we are in Christ Jesus.

- We were created in God's image.
- God created us with purpose.
- We are his masterpiece.
- According to Jeremiah 1:5 (KJV), "He knew thee before thou camest out of the womb."
- We are children of the most high God.
- We are new creatures in Christ Jesus.
- We are a peculiar people in the Lord.

- We are the apple of God's eye.

- God loves you and I so much that, according to John 3:16 (KJV), "… God so loved the world, that he gave his only begotten Son, that whosoever believe in him should not perish, but have everlasting life."

That's how special you and I are to God

Young Ladies, You Can Survive

Some young women think that because a guy has been supporting them for a long time, they won't be able to support themselves or their children if the guy leaves them. That's not true. I am letting you know that "with God All things are possible" (Matthew 19:26). With God you can survive. With God you can make it. With God you will succeed. With God you can raise your kids. With God you are protected. So I'm not talking about making it by your own strength but by the strength of the Lord. Zechariah 4:6 (KJV) says, "It not by our might nor by power, but by the Lord Spirit." And that is the Word. Do you know that the God of this universe knows how to take care of his sons and daughters? But he will do so only if people will allow him to; Jesus is a gentleman.

When Jesus saved me, I found my true love in Jesus Christ. Seek and give your heart to the Lord, and you won't go wrong.

> True love won't leave you,
>
> True love won't hurt you,
>
> True love won't fail you,
>
> True love won't kill you.
>
> True love will take care of you,
>
> True love will help you,
>
> True love will deliver you,

True love will save you.

Seek Jesus Christ, the true love, and you won't go wrong.

Matthew 7:7 (KJV) says, "Ask, and it shall be given you; seek, and ye shall find; knock and it shall be open unto you."

I am here to share with you how much we are loved by God.

We are so loved by God "that he created us in his own image," according to Genesis 1:27 (KJV).

We are so loved by God "that we are his workmanship created in Christ Jesus unto good works," according to Ephesians 2:10 (KJV).

We are so loved by God that he is protecting us. Jesus said, "No weapon that is formed against thee/us shall prosper and every tongue that shall rise against thee in judgement thou shalt condemn" (Isaiah 54:17 KJV).

We are so loved by God that, "we have redemption through his blood the forgivingness of sin," according to Ephesians 1:7 (KJV).

We are so loved by God that "Jesus was wounded for our transgressions he was bruised for our iniquities: the chastisement of our peace was upon him; and with his stripes we are healed," according to Isaiah 53:5 (KJV).

And we are so loved by God, according to John 3:16 (KJV), that "… God so loved the world that he gave his only begotten Son, that whosoever believeth in him should not perish, but have everlasting life."

That's why we know we are loved by God.

Life Lesson in Training Up a Child

Moms and dads, I am here to let you know that having a baby is a lot of responsibility and a lot of work. It takes more than just having a child; it takes showing your child love, protecting your child, and being there for the child. Also, it takes providing for your child and raising your child up in the Lord. Talk to and teach your kids and teenagers, because if you don't, the world will. For example, we are living in a world where people are calling right wrong and wrong right. We are living in a world where people want to see anything go. We are living in a world where people are living any way they choose. So I believe talking to your kids is necessary. Believe it or not, your opinion does matter to them; I don't care how much a child thinks he or she knows it all. No child knows everything; that's why the Word says, in Proverbs 22:6 (KJV), "Train up a child in the way he should go: and when he is old, he will not depart from it." You train them up; they don't train you. Don't beat them down with words; lift them up and tell them how they can do better. You train them, you talk to them, you love on them, and you show them. It's better if you can communicate with your children so you can help them in many ways, no matter what your differences. Maintain your relationship with them.

Real Talk 1

I learned that the Lord never left me!

I have to tell you this. When I was out on the streets, God did not let me die in my sin. He was protecting me all along while I was in my mess. I did not know this until he showed me it was him keeping me. He could have taken me right there in my sin. He could have said "Enough!" and then I would not be here. He saw beyond my mess and didn't turn his back on me. He received me with his open arms an forgave me. He showed me his love all along and cared for my soul. God did it for me, and he can do the same for you. Jesus cares for your soul too. I learned that the Lord never left me; he was with me all the way.

Real Talk 2

The world will tell us it's okay to live any way we choose to live. But God wants us to walk into truth and not a lie. Now, the world going to tell us it's okay to do this and it's okay to do that, but it's not okay according to the Word of God. For example, the world tells us it's okay to have sex long as we protect ourselves. Now, the world is not going to tell you that In 1 Corinthians 6:18 (KJV), the Word says, "Flee fornication. Every sin that a man doeth is without the body: but he that committed fornication sinneth against his own body." Also, I wanted to share with you that Proverbs 14:12 (KJV) says, "There is a way which seemeth right unto a man, but the end thereof is the ways of death." And this is the truth. What is truth? God's Word is truth. God wants his children to walk truth and not a lie.

I want to share another truth with you. God loves us so much that he shares truth with us through his Word. We are born into a world of sin, and we don't have to continue to live blind to sin. For instance, we are *in* this world but not *of* the world; the world taught me how to go against my Father God's Word. Now, if I didn't know much about my Father's Word and I didn't spend time with my Father God and take heed, I would think the world was right. What I am trying to say here is that the world can't teach me how to live in a holy way, the world can't teach me how to live righteously, and the world can't teach us how to live for God. The world *can* teach us how to sin and go against God and his Word. If people truly knew the Word of God, they would be trying to live for God and not for flesh. We don't have to continue to live in bondage, as Jesus Christ has already set us free. John 8:36 (KJV) says, "If the Son therefore shall make you free, ye shall be free indeed."

When we are walking in truth and living according to the Word of God, our lives will change for the better in Jesus's name. I want people to know we have choices down here on this earth. We can choose to live for the world, or we can choose to live for God. We can choose to live in a godly way or we can choose to live in an ungodly way. The decision to make wise choices is up to us. We have instructions that we can live by on the earth—the Word of God. God gives us opportunities to live better lives here on this earth before going into the heavenly realm. And the opportunities that he gives us are not harmful; they are helpful and very beneficial to us. We are so blessed to have the Word of God on this earth and a chance to learn and walk in truth.

What Do "Ungodly" and "Godly" Mean?

According to *Strong's Concordance*, "ungodly" means "Impious or wicked: ungodly man." In other words, when a person is living in an ungodly way, that person is disobeying God. But we have a savior that is willing to help us turn from our wicked ways if we want to live in a godly way. Roman 5:6 (KJV) says, "For when we were yet without strength, in due time Christ died for the ungodly." I thank God we have a savior.

In addition to that, Psalm 1:1–6 (KJV) says, "Blessed is the man that walketh not in the counsel of the ungodly, nor standeth in the way of sinners, nor sitteth in the seat of the scornful." The ungodly are not so: but are like the chaff which the wind driveth away. Therefore the ungodly shall not stand in the judgment, nor sinners in the congregation of the righteous. For the Lord knoweth the way of the righteous: but the ungodly shall perish."

According to *Strong's Concordance*, "godly" means "piously; godly." When a person is living in a godly way, that person is obeying God and living according to the

Word of God. Now, when a person walks in obeying God, he or she gets rewarded for being obedient. As a result, a person will have blessings bestowed upon him or her and will have a closer walk with God. In the book of John 14:21 (KJV), Jesus says, "He that hath my commandments, and keepeth them, he it is that loveth me: and he that loveth me shall be loved of my Father, and I will love him and will manifest myself to him." And this is a true blessing from our Lord.

Also, Hebrews 12:28 (KJV) says, "Wherefore we receiving a kingdom which cannot be moved, let us have grace, whereby we may serve God acceptably with reverence and godly fear." I believe that when we walk in obedience, God blesses us in many ways. Not only do we get blessed, but our obedience blesses others as well. And that's the truth

Who Said?

Who said Jesus is not real? John 3:16 (KJV) says, "For God so loved the world that he gave his only begotten son that whosoever believe in him should not perish but have everlasting life." You and I are alive today because Jesus lives. This is how real Jesus is.

Who said Jesus is not Lord? Jesus Christ is Lord over my life, and a great one too. Philippians 2:11 (KJV) says, "And that every tongue should confess that Jesus Christ is Lord, to the glory of God the Father." He is the King of Kings and the Lord of Lords.

Who said Jesus has not kept them? Genesis 2:7 (KJV) states that man became a living soul when the Lord blew on him. We have no breath without the Lord.

Who said Jesus cant healed? Isaiah 53:5 (KJV) tells me that Jesus is my healer. And Jesus can be your healer too.

Who said Jesus doesn't give second chances? Jesus gave us another chance "when he said Father forgive them for they know not what they do" (Luke23:34 KJV).

Who said Jesus doesn't save? The devil is a liar. Jesus saved my life and yours too; that's why we are all here today. John 3:17 (KJV) states that "Jesus came not to condemn but through him the world might be saved."

Who said Jesus doesn't protect? That's why many of us exist today whether you want to believe it or not, it was Jesus that protected us in our mess. Romans 5:8 (KJV) states, "In yet we were sinners Christ died and rose for us." He sends warnings throughout the day. He is our protector.

Jesus Is Real

I want to share with you that there is a real Lord, Father God, and Holy Ghost, and they are not a fairytale. God loves us with an everlasting love, and "he don't wish that any should perish." That's why he sent his only begotten Son, Jesus Christ, to die on the cross for us and to rise for us so we can live unto him and not ourselves. Now when God looks at us he sees us through the blood of Jesus Christ. Jesus Christ, the Savior whom I speak about, wants to share his Word with us so we can live holy lives on this earth before we get to the kingdom of God. The Lord wants to bless his people; that's why he gives us clear instructions through his Word so we can follow. The Good Shepherd said, "my sheep know my voice and a stranger they will not follow." Jesus Christ is the Good Shepherd that laid his life down for the sheep. And Jesus Christ can be your Good Shepherd too. He is a real Lord, Father God, and Holy Ghost and they are not a fairytale.

Jesus Is a Lover

It's a better way of living and it's in accordance with the Word of God. I want younger and older people to know they don't have to look for love on the outside. The true love I am talking about is the love they can find in Jesus Christ. You can seek this true love, and you won't go wrong. This love I am talking about is agape love, "the contrasted with eros, philia, unconditional love" the love that Jesus gives. This is the true love here.

This is the agape love,

Agape, which is the highest form of love.

It's neither fake nor phony.

This is not a misleading or deceitful love.

This is not saying I love you and not acting upon it.

This is not saying I love you only

today and not tomorrow.

This is a true, genuine agape love that God gives.

This is an unconditional love,

Where God loves us in spite of our faults,

Where God loves us in spite of our mistakes,

Where God loves us in spite of our failures.

This love is a keeper's love.

This love is a Shepherd's love

This love here is a Father's true, genuine love.

Agape love.

Jesus is a lover.

We Can Change Our Diets to Healthy Spiritual Ones

Teenagers and young adults, we can change our worldly diets to healthy spiritual ones. A person doesn't have to stay stuck in having a worldly diet. There is hope. We don't have to continue to feed off the flesh; we can look to our spiritual provider for help to get us the daily nourishment that we need. Jesus is the nutrients that we need to be feeding off of; we can do that by reading the Word of God, praying, and seeking God's face. Proverbs 4:20–22 (KJV) says, "My son, attend to my words; incline thine ear unto my sayings. Let them not depart from thine eyes; keep them in the midst of thine heart. For they are life unto those that find them and health to all their flesh." I want you to know that having a spiritual appetite is good and feeding on the Word of God is delicious. Psalm 34:8 (KJV) says, "O taste and see that the Lord is good: blessed is the man that trust in him."

Don't Waste or Abuse It

Life is a gift.

Life is precious.

Life is valuable.

So don't waste or abuse it.

Enjoy your life in the Lord

The gift that God has given us is so precious; the gift that God blessed us with is Jesus Christ. Cherish him, honor him, praise him, and give in to him. Give honor to whom honor is due. Live your life to please him.

When I heard of Jesus,

When I got introduced to Jesus Christ,

This man name Jesus saved my life, healed my body,

and

Gave me hope

When I didn't have any hope.

When the Lord touched me,

He changed my life for the better.

He healed my body,

He raised me up,

and

He saved my soul.

Here is some scripture that I would like to share with you that will help you with your relationship with Jesus

> For God so loved the world, that he gave his only begotten Son, that whosoever beliveth in him should not perish, but have everlasting life. (John 3:16 KJV)

> If we confess our sins he is faithful and just to forgive us our sins, and to cleanse us from all unrighteousness. (1 John 1:9 KJV)

> Love not the world, neither the things that are in the world. If any man loves the world, the love of the Father is not in him. 16. "For all that is in the world, the lust of the flesh, and the lust of the eyes, and the pride of life, is not of the Father, but is of the world. (1 John 2:15–16 KJV)

We are of God: he that knoweth God heareth us; he that is not of God hearth not us. Hereby know we the spirit of truth, and the spirit of error. (1 John 4:6 KJV)

What? Know ye not that your body is the temple of the Holy Ghost which is in you, which ye have of God, and ye are not your own. For ye are bought with a price: therefore glorify God in your body, and in your spirit, which are God's. (1 Corinthians 6:19–20KJV)

I say therefore to the unmarried and widows, It is good for them if they abide even as him. But if they cannot contain, let them marry: for it is better to marry than to burn. (1 Corinthians 7:8–9 KJV)

I want to share with you the one I service, the Lord. Jesus Christ is someone that can help you through all your situations. He is someone that you can run to and talk to. He will not speak negatively about you, he will not hurt you, and he will never put you down. And I know that he can help you through any of your situations, because he helped me. Yes, his name is Jesus Christ. Romans 2:11 (KJV) says, "For there is no respect of persons with God." And that's the Word. You can tell him anything. There is a reason and purpose for everything you go through. Even if you made a mistake, he can turn that mistake around for your good. So you don't have to beat yourself up; I know that you can give anything and everything to him because In Isaiah 9:6(KJV) says, "Jesus is called the Wonderful Counselor, The mighty God, The everlasting Father, The Prince of

Peace and he has the government on his shoulder." So if Jesus has the government on his shoulders, you and I know that he can handle anything and in our lives. Nothing is too big or too small for him to handle.

Reflections

What valuable lessons did you learn from chapter 4?

_____

_____

_____

_____

What is the highest form of love that God loves us with?
What does this mean to you?

_____

_____

_____

_____

CHAPTER 5
Salvation

Repentance refers to the action of repenting, sincere regret, or remorse. According to the KJV Bible, repentance is a call to persons to make a radical turn from one way of life to another. Also, *The New Unger's Bible Dictionary* states that repentance means a "change" of mind. Repentance is something we all should embrace in our daily lives. We can't only say that we repent; we also have to walk in repentance. One of the ways we can do this is by confessing our sins. As 1 John 1:9 (KJV) states, "If we confess our sins, he is faithful and just to forgive us our sins, and to cleanse us from all unrighteousness."

Confession

"Confess" means "admit or state that one has committed a crime or is at fault in some way." According to *The New Unger's Bible Dictionary*, "confession" relates to acknowledging one's sins. "It is also used in the sense of yielding or change of one's convictions."

A part of repentance is asking for forgiveness. Some people may ask, "Why do I need to ask God to forgive me?" We all need God to forgive us, as we all have sin. Now, I know that no one is perfect but Jesus Christ. The one who came down from heaven died on the cross and rose on the third day with all power. He is the perfect one, and we are imperfect people. We need Jesus Christ, even if we don't think that we have done anything wrong or sinned. We have all fallen short of the glory of God. Romans 3:23 (KJV) says, "For all have sinned, and come short of the glory of God." And this is the Word. We all need to ask God to forgive us! In the book of John, the Word states, "If we say that we have no sin, we deceive ourselves, and the truth is not in us."

I am here to let you know salvation takes more than being a good person. It is not achieved by works, according to Ephesians 2:8–9 (KJV): "For by grace are ye saved through faith; and that not of yourselves: it is a gift of God. Not of works, lest any man should boast." It's important that we repent.

Now that you have heard the Word of God, what are you going to do?

Salvation

Salvation refers to deliverance from sin and its consequences; it is believed by Christians to be brought about by faith in Jesus Christ.

I wanted to share this with you too, when Jesus Christ saved me. I began to see things in a different way, with a different outlook. I even saw a lot more clearly than I had when I was walking in darkness. Even my spiritual lens got brighter and lighter for me. It was a change for the better. I wouldn't change it for the world. I didn't want to live the same old type of lifestyle that I lived before. My body got better; my tune had changed. I didn't want to sin against my Lord God. I wanted to do all that I could to please my Lord God.

If you would like to dedicate your life to the Lord, you can do that right now, right where you are. Romans10:9–11 (KJV) says "that if thou shalt confess with thy mouth the Lord Jesus, shalt believe in thine heart that God hath raised him from the dead, thou shalt be saved. For with the heart man believeth unto righteousness; and with the mouth confession is made unto salvation. For the scripture saith, Whosoever believeth on him shall not be ashamed." The Lord Jesus Christ will come into your life, and you will never be the same. Jesus Christ will change your life for the better too.

If you accepted Jesus Christ as your savior, then you can write your name_____, the date_____, and the time_____ here as a reminder of this important life-changing decision you made. If you want more information concerning your decision you made, You can contact me at nieasia411@yahoo.com, and I can refer you to a pastor at a local church.

When we have given our lives over to Jesus Christ, it does not mean that we are perfect people or that we have arrived anywhere. We have to ask God to help us to walk pleasingly in his sight, because the Word says, "… for all have sinned and come short of the glory of God." We must do this amid the temptations that come our way even when we are babes in Christ. We don't want to go back to the same old lifestyle of living that we came out of, and we don't have to keep backsliding either. Jesus Christ does expect us to be obedient children to our Father God and him. That why it's so important to establish a personal relationship with Jesus Christ, Father God, and the Holy Ghost. I am not only talking about going to church on Sundays or even going to a church building; I am talking about spending quality time with Jesus Christ and Father God by being in his Word. You can learn his ways by reading the Bible and then walking in it. Also, being obedient to him is one of the ways we can please him. Learn what Jesus likes and what he dislikes. Jesus Christ is real, and he walks in truth. Also, I am talking about praying, praising, and worshipping Jesus Christ, as well as Father God (in Jesus's mighty name). I am here to let you know that if we are living for Jesus Christ, we are going to go through some things. One thing I do know is that he didn't bring us this far to leave us. In Deuteronomy 31:6 (KJV) says, "Jesus will never leave us nor forsake us." That means we are not alone in this walk, and Romans 8:31 (KJV) says, "if God be for us, who can be against us." We have the victorious one with us. We have the powerful one with us. We have our Savior with us, and he loves us so much that he shares truth with us.

Purpose

I would like to share some questions and scriptures that will give you a clearer understanding of God's purpose for your life. Do you know that you have a purpose here on this earth? There is a purpose behind everything you go through in this life. There is a purpose behind the mess.

You may be asking, "Why am I here? Why does it seem I can't just make it? Why am I in an environment where it seems I'm not going anywhere? Is there any hope for me? I want to let you know that you and I were created for a greater purpose, and yes, there is hope for us.

To help you know and grow more, following are some scriptures the Lord blessed me with that can also bless you.

For I know the thoughts that I think toward you, saith the Lord, thoughts of peace, and not of evil, to give you an expected end. (Jeremiah 29:11 KJV)

Why art thou cast down, O my soul? And why art thou disquieted within me? Hope thou in God: for I shall yet praise him, who is the health of my countenance, and my God. (Psalm 42:11 KJV)

says, " Let Israel hope in the Lord: for with the Lord there is mercy, and with him is plenteous redemption." Psalm 130:7 (KJV)

Now faith is the substance of things hoped for, the evidence of things not seen. (Hebrews 11:1KJV)

Now the God of hope fill you with all joy and peace in believing, that ye may abound in hope, through the power of the Holy Ghost. (Romans 15:13 KJV)

"Purpose" relates to the reason for which something is done or created, or for which something exists. You and I have a purpose. We have a greater purpose than we can ever imagine. Each and every person on this earth has a purpose, whether he or she knows it or not. We were created with purpose by the Master's hands. Ephesians 2:10 (KJV) says, "For we are his workmanship, created in Christ Jesus unto good works, which God hath before ordained that we should walk in them." And that's the Word.

CPSIA information can be obtained
at www.ICGtesting.com
Printed in the USA
BVHW050715041122
651123BV00001B/49